KIDCHAT

QUESTIONS TO FUEL
YOUNG MINDS AND MOUTHS

Bret Nicholaus and Paul Lowrie
The Question Guys™
Authors of the national bestseller *The Conversation Piece*

QUESTMARC Publishing,
a division of QUESTMARC Entertainment

QUESTMARC
Entertainment / Publishing
P.O. Box 340
Yankton, SD 57078

© 2001 Bret Nicholaus and Paul Lowrie

Illustrations by Scott Luken
(P.O. Box 159 • Yankton, SD 57078)

Cover and text design by Donna Bollich

ATTENTION: SCHOOLS AND BUSINESSES

Questmarc books are available at quantity discounts with bulk purchase for educational, business, or promotional use. For more information, contact:
Questmarc Publishing, Special Sales Department,
P.O. Box 340, Yankton, South Dakota 57078.

ISBN #0-9634251-6-1

Library of Congress Catalog Card Number: 2001087029

Printed in the United States of America

First Edition: April 2001

10 9 8 7 6 5 4 3 2

KIDCHAT

WELCOME

KidChat? What exactly is this book all about, you may be wondering. Simply put, *KidChat* is a collection of hundreds of entertaining questions that promote creative thinking and thought-provoking conversations among kids...and between kids and their parents. In other words, in addition to giving kids plenty of food for thought, this book gives them plenty of food for *talk*!

Kids will absolutely love using this book with their friends, as it facilitates fun discussions about things they probably don't think about every day, and in fact may *never* have thought about in the past. It can be used at school with their peers or in the home with their parents. It works equally well at the dinner table and on long trips in the car. It's a favorite for sleepovers, parties, and children's groups, and is an ideal tool for creative writing. Many students have even encouraged their teachers to read a "Question of the Day" to get the morning started in the classroom.

There is no particular order to the questions, so kids can open to any page at any time and read whatever question they see there. And of course, there are no wrong answers to these questions—only opinions. Often times, kids will discover that the way they think changes from day to day; the answer given for a question today may be completely different from their answer to the same question tomorrow.

Regardless of when, where or how *KidChat* is used, one thing is certain: Kids (as well as parents) will have oodles of fun giving their responses to the questions...and in the process they'll learn an amazing amount about themselves and others.

Bret Nicholaus and Paul Lowrie,
The Question Guys™

Special Note

Every 15 questions or so, kids will notice a heading that says "IMAGINATION IGNITER." These words indicate that the question below it is specially designed to stimulate *very* creative thinking and the "full-blown" use of their imagination.

"I resent the limitations
of my own imagination."

—Walt Disney

1

If something besides rain or snow could fall occasionally from the sky, what would you want it to be? (Example: Jellybeans.)

2

If you could be shrunk down to one inch tall for a day, what do you think would be the most exciting place to explore?

IMAGINATION IGNITER

3

If you were asked to help design a new roller coaster for a popular amusement park, what unique and fun features would you suggest for the new ride?

4

If you could invite anyone in the world to come to your school and give a talk in front of the students, whom would you invite to your school?

5

If you had to work on a farm for one week during the summer, what particular job or chore do you think would be the most fun to do?

6

If you had a secret club for your friends and had to come up with a password that everyone would have to say before they could come in for your "meetings," what password would members of the club have to say?

7

Suppose that whenever you wanted to get away from everyone you could simply blink your eyes three times and be anywhere else in the world. Where would you want to go whenever you felt the need to get away?

8

If you could make anything at all twice as big as it already is, what would you double in size?

9

What particular quality above all others do you look for when choosing your friends?

10

If you could ride your bike safely around and through any city in the world, what city would you choose?

11

What is one thing you are pretty certain you will be quite good at when you are an adult?

12

If you could jump into a time machine and travel back in time to any moment in history, what historical moment would you want to witness?

What is the silliest thing you've ever done?

Which of your favorite foods would be the most difficult for you to give up completely for one full year?

What musical instrument do you think would best describe your personality?

8

16

If you could do anything you wanted—anything at all—for your next birthday, what would you do?

17

If, instead of riding to school in a car or bus, you could be taken to and from school each day in any unusual vehicle or piece of machinery, what would you choose for your form of transportation? (Examples: A tractor, a firetruck, a bulldozer, etc.)

IMAGINATION IGNITER

18

If you had to become one of the following eight birds for a week, from your first choice to last choice how would you rank our feathered friends?
(Choices: Cardinal, eagle, flamingo, ostrich, parrot, peacock, penguin, and seagull.)

19

What is one thing many of your friends seem to like that you really *don't* like?

20

If you won $1,000 as part of a contest, how would you spend the money?

21

If, whenever you turned on a drinking fountain, you could get any drink of your choice to spout up, what drink do you think you'd choose most often?

22

If you could create the perfect weather day, mixing together in one day any and all elements of weather that you like, how would the day unfold? (Example: Snow in the morning, sunny and hot in the afternoon, and a thunderstorm at night.)

23

What is your favorite month of the year? Why?

24

If you could be any animal for one day, living in its environment and doing whatever that particular animal does during a typical day, which animal would you be?

25

What are three specific things that you believe make our country such a great nation to live in?

26

If you could change three things about our country that would help to make it a better nation than it is, what changes would you make?

14

27

If you had been a kid living in the 1800s, over 100 years ago, what aspect of life do you think would have been the most difficult?

28

If you could jump off any high object in the world and be assured of a safe landing, what thing would you want to jump off of?

29

If you could become extremely knowledgeable on any subject simply by snapping your fingers, which subject would you choose?

If you could grow up in any town other than the one you currently live in, which town would you choose?

If you had to move to another state, which state would you want it to be?

If you had to live in a different country for one month, which country would you choose?

IMAGINATION IGNITER

33

If you were asked to write a book that would be sold in bookstores across the country, what would your story be about?

34

If you could change one thing about your favorite holiday, what change would you make?

35

What part of a typical day do you look forward to the most?

36

If you had plenty of time and money (and your parents' permission), how would you decorate the outside of your home at Christmas?

37

In your opinion, what animal makes the funniest or most unusual sound?

38

Other than either of your parents, who is one adult that you really have a lot of fun with? Why?

39

Suppose that instead of having a name, you had a number, and people would always refer to you as that number. What number—besides #1—would you want to take the place of your name? (Examples: #8, #100, #999, etc.)

40

What is one subject currently not being taught in school that you would love to see added to your learning experience?

41

Who is one person you've read or heard about in history that you think would have been very fun to meet?

42

If you knew you could win a first-place trophy in any one event or contest you decided to enter, which event would you choose?

43

If you could choose one vegetable that you would never, ever have to eat again, which vegetable would it be?

44

When a new friend comes over to your house, what is one of the first things that you love to show them or share with them?

If you owned a candy store, what would be your favorite kind of candy to sell?

If you could have one superpower, what would you want it to be?

What is the best vacation you've ever taken? What made it so great?

IMAGINATION IGNITER

48

If you could create a brand-new flavor of ice cream, mixing anything into it that you want, what kind of ice cream would it be?

49

If you could train any wild animal to be a good house pet, what animal would you choose for your pet?

50

If your hair had to be a different color than it actually is, what color would you want it to be?

51

What is your favorite thing to talk about when you are with your friends?

52

What particular food is your favorite part of Thanksgiving dinner?

53

If you could give yourself a new first name, what name would you choose?

54

If your picture could appear on the cover of any magazine, what magazine's cover would you want to be on?

55

If snow could fall in any flavor, what flavor would you choose?

56

If just one time snow could fall in a color other than white, what color would you want the snow to be?

57

What is your favorite sound?

58

If you had to spend an entire weekend, day and night, living in any store of your choice, what store would you want to stay in?

59

If Halloween were tomorrow, what would you want to dress up as?

60

What particular aspect of being an adult are you looking forward to the most?

61

What is something most adults do that seems really silly to you?

62

If you could somehow jump into the television set and actually experience, along with the TV characters, what's happening in the show, what particular program would you want to be a part of?

63

If you could add any really interesting feature to your bicycle, what would it be?

64

If you could live in any large or famous building in the world, what building would be your home?

65

If you could have 25 of anything in the world, what would you choose?

66

If you were asked to create a large swimming pool for all the kids that live in your town, what special features would you be sure that this pool had?

67

What is the most exciting tunnel that you've ever been through? What is the most exciting bridge that you've ever gone over?

68

If you could know the secret behind any magic trick, which one would you want to know?

69

What are three jobs that you think might be really fun to have some-day?

70

In your opinion, what is the most annoying sound?

71

If you could change one rule that your parents have set for you, what one would you change?

72.

If you could add anything at all to the typical mall that would make it far more exciting or interesting to visit, what would you add?

73

If you could have any famous person's autograph, whose would you want most of all?

74

If you could teach any animal a brand-new trick, what animal would you choose and what trick would you teach it?

75

If you opened up a restaurant, what would you name the place and what type of food would your restaurant serve?

76

What do you think would be the scariest or most dangerous job to have?

77

If you knew that beginning tomorrow you would be blind for one full year, what would you want to be sure to see today while you still had time?

78

What is your favorite day of the year? Why?

79

What is your favorite thing that begins with the letter "L"?

IMAGINATION IGNITER

80

If you were asked to create a new and exciting exhibit for a large zoo, what type of exhibit would you build and what would be some of its most interesting features?

81

If you and a few of your best friends could have any place in the world completely to yourselves for one day, what would you choose? (Examples: An amusement park or a movie theater.)

82

If you knew that beginning tomorrow you would be deaf for one full year, what would you want to be sure to hear today while you still had time?

83

What is something really extraordinary you think you would like to achieve or accomplish during your lifetime? (Example: Climbing a famous mountain.)

84

If you lived in the country and were given a horse as your pet, what would you name it?

85

What is your all-time-favorite song? Why?

86

If you had to give up all of your CDs except one, which one would you be sure to keep?

87

If you could personally meet any professional athlete, whom would you want to meet most of all?

88

If you could ask the president of the United States one question, knowing that you would get an honest answer, what question would you ask him?

89

If you were given 5,000 ping-pong balls, what would you do with them?

90

If, from the moment you got up until the moment you went to bed, you could do anything you wanted for one full day, where would you go and what would you do to make it a truly perfect day?

91

If you could be a modern-day explorer, what specific part of the world would you want to explore?

92.

If you could be in the crowd to watch a professional try a dangerous stunt during the filming of a movie, what stunt would you like to see performed?

93

If you could add a brand-new holiday to the calendar, what would you want the new holiday to be and how would people celebrate it?

IMAGINATION IGNITER

94

If you had to create an all-new vacation destination, where would it be located and what would it be like?

95

If you could know just one thing about your own future, what would you want to know?

96

What is your favorite commercial on television right now?

97

If you could break any world record you wanted, which one would you choose?

98

What is the most exciting thing you've ever seen in person?

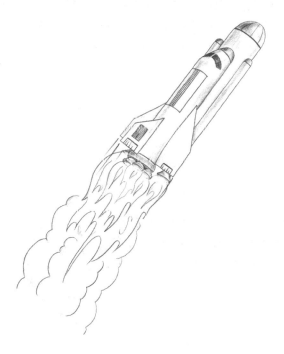

99

Would you rather live in a large, busy city with lots of tall buildings, shops and people, or out in the country where you would have farms, animals and wide-open spaces?

100

What is the most interesting or exciting thing you've learned this year in school?

What is your all-time-favorite scene from a movie?

If you could do something really heroic, what would you do?

If you could avoid any household chore for the rest of your life, what chore would it be?

104

If you could be a part of a large parade, what would you want to be doing in the parade?

105

What musical instrument's sound is your favorite? Why?

106

If you could have free tickets to any sports event in the world, what would you want to see?

107

If you were walking down your street and found a box that was sealed up and marked with the words "Do Not Open," what would you do?

108

If you could be lifted high above the ground to see anything you wanted just like a bird would see it, what would you want to see from the air?

109

If you were asked to write an article for your city's newspaper, what subject would you want to write about and what would the headline say?

110

If you could paint a giant mural on one entire wall in your bedroom, what scene or images would you paint?

111

What is the best gift you ever received? Why?

112

If you could open up your own store in the local mall, what would you sell in it?

113

What is something you once saw or did that made you laugh extremely hard and long?

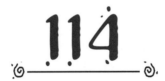

114

If you could create what you consider to be the perfect ice-cream sundae, what would your creamy concoction be like?

115

If you could choose one place that you would never again have to visit, what place would it be?

116

If you knew that all the people in the area would be safe, would you rather witness a volcano erupting or a tidal wave hitting the shore?

117

If you could be any type of bug or insect for one day, what type would you be?

118

What is the latest you've ever stayed up at night? Why?

119

Besides things that you absolutely must have in order to live—like food and water—what would be the hardest thing for you to go without for 30 days? (Example: Your favorite video game.)

120

If you could choose right now exactly how tall you will be when you are all finished growing, how tall would you want to be?

If you were creating a movie about toys coming to life, what type of toy would be the main character?

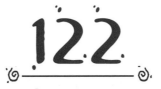

Suppose that in addition to Monday through Friday, you had to attend school for 30 Saturdays...but as a result you would get an extra month off during summer vacation. How would you feel about an arrangement like that?

IMAGINATION IGNITER

123

If you were asked to create a new park for the city or town that you live in, what would be some of the features of this new place where kids and adults would gather?

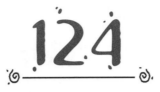

When was the last time you did something really nice for your parents? What is one thing you could do very soon for them that would make them really happy?

If you were going to visit a large museum, what type of exhibit more than any other would you hope to see there?

126

Who is your all-time-favorite cartoon character? Why?

127

If you could be famous for anything at all, what would you want to be famous for?

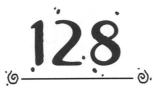

128

If you had to list the following treats from one to ten, with one being your favorite and ten being your least favorite in the list, how would you rank them? (Choices: Cake, cookies, donuts, hamburgers, hot dogs, ice cream, pizza, popcorn, potato chips and watermelon.)

129

What is the hardest test you've ever taken in school?

130

Think with your nose for a moment: Which of the four seasons has the best smells, both outdoors and indoors?

In your opinion, what is the greatest thing ever invented? Why?

How many days have you been alive so far? How many hours? How many minutes? (If you need help to figure this out, just ask an adult.)

Besides opening gifts, what is your favorite thing to do or see during the Christmas season?

134

If you could change one thing about school—and only one thing—what would you change?

135

Would you rather be able to jump long and high like a kangaroo or climb trees effortlessly like a monkey?

136

What is one event you've seen only on television that you would just love to actually be a part of someday? (Example: Attending the Super Bowl.)

137

What are you most curious to learn about as you get older?

IMAGINATION IGNITER

138

If you were crowned king or queen and could have a castle built for you, what are some features you would want your castle to have?

If you were king or queen, what is the first rule that you would set for the people in your kingdom?

If you could take a running jump into a pool filled with any objects, liquid, or substance of your choice, what would you want the pool to be filled with? (Example: Grape jelly.)

141

If you could start a collection of anything you wanted, what would it be?

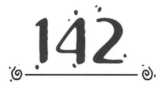

142

If you could have a year's supply of cotton candy in any color and flavor of your choice, what color and flavor would you want?

143

What is the most interesting book you've ever read? What made it so interesting for you?

144

If you could take only one trip in a time machine, would you rather travel into the future to see what life *will* be like or would you rather travel back into the past to see what life *was* like?

145

If you could choose any person's
face to appear on a new dollar bill,
what person's face would you choose?

76

146

What is your favorite ornament that hangs each year on the family Christmas tree?

147

If you could decorate a tree in your house for another holiday besides Christmas, what holiday would it be, how would you decorate the tree, and what color lights would you use?

148

What is one problem you see in our own country or in the world that you hope is resolved by the time you become an adult?

149

If you met a 100-year-old person and could ask them one question about their life, what would you be most curious to find out?

150

If you could have the voice of any famous person, whose voice would you want to have?

151

If, instead of a buzzer or music, your alarm clock could wake you up every morning by releasing one of your favorite smells, what smell would you choose?

152

Whenever you are having a bad day, what is the best thing you can do to help cheer yourself up?

153

What is the best joke you've ever heard?

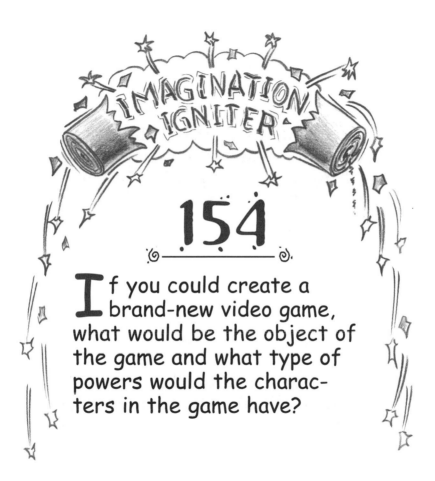

IMAGINATION IGNITER

154

If you could create a brand-new video game, what would be the object of the game and what type of powers would the characters in the game have?

If you could "jump into" the pages of any book and actually experience everything that's happening in the story, what book would you choose?

How do you imagine that you will look physically when you are about 21 years old?

If you were given one minute on national television to say or do anything you wanted, what would you say or do for those 60 seconds?

If you could somehow combine the sounds of any two musical instruments to create a brand-new sound in music, which two instruments' sounds would you mix?

159

If you could take a train ride across any of the seven continents, which continent would you want to see most of all? (Choices: Africa, Antarctica, Asia, Australia, Europe, North America and South America.)

160

What is your favorite song from a TV show? What is your favorite song from a movie?

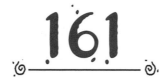

161

When you have free time just to lie back and daydream, what do you think about more often than anything else?

162

What object in the sky or outer space is the most fascinating to you? (Examples: Asteroids, moon, planets, stars, sun, etc.)

163

If you could make anything at all go faster, what would you choose?

164

If you could make anything at all go slower, what would you choose?

165

If you could draw or sketch professionally, what do you think would be the general theme of your drawings? (Example: Dogs.)

166

In your opinion, what is the most beautiful animal in the world? What animal do you think is the ugliest?

167

What is your least favorite thing to do every morning before you leave for school?

IMAGINATION IGNITER

168

If you had to pick a punctuation mark as a symbol of who you are and what your personality is, which mark would you choose? (Examples: Question mark, period, comma, colon, exclamation point, quotation marks, etc.)

169

What hat state that you haven't yet visited are you most interested in seeing?

170

If f you had a pet parrot and could teach it to say any word or short sentence, what would you teach the beaked blabbermouth to say?

171

If you could get rid of one color completely, what color would it be?

172

What do you forget to do more often than anything else?

If you could somehow take a geographic feature from another state and move it very close to your own town, what geographic feature would you like to move? (Example: Moving the Grand Canyon from Arizona to a location near you.)

Besides your mom or dad, who is one adult you feel comfortable talking to when you have a problem or concern about something in your life?

175

I f you were a tree, what type would you want to be, where would you want to grow, and what would be your favorite month of the year?

176

If you were a mouse loose in somebody's house, what type of bait would draw you quickly toward the trap? (Example: A piece of pizza.)

177

If you could change one thing about your bedroom, what would you change? (The change you make can be big or small.)

178

If you could have starred in any movie, what movie would it be?

179

If you could take any holiday and make it last two days instead of just one, which holiday would you pick?

180

If you could represent our country in the Olympic Games, what sport or event would you want to compete in?

181

What is something you and your parents could do together each night at the table that would make dinnertime more interesting for everyone?
(Example: Having everyone around the table give their answer to a question in this book.)

182

Besides your real birthday, what is one other date on the calendar that you think would have been a great day to be born?

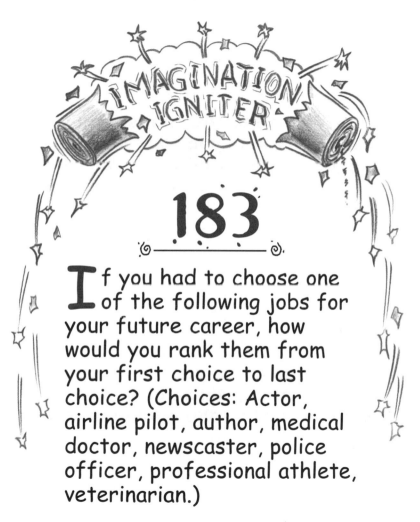

IMAGINATION IGNITER

183

If you had to choose one of the following jobs for your future career, how would you rank them from your first choice to last choice? (Choices: Actor, airline pilot, author, medical doctor, newscaster, police officer, professional athlete, veterinarian.)

184

If the doorbell to your house could make any sound you wanted it to make, what noise would you want to hear whenever the button was pushed?

185

If you were given a camera and a roll of film and then told you could take pictures of anything you wanted, what would you want to photograph most of all?

In your opinion, what is the most boring thing to do? What is something you could do to make it more exciting?

If you were in a trivia contest, what category do you think you would do best in?

If you could invent anything you wanted, what would it be?

!89

If you could make a giant fruit salad for yourself that was filled with any four fruits, which four fruits would you mix together in your salad?

190

When you meet other kids for the first time, what is one thing you usually want to know right away about them?

191

If you were asked to rename your town, what new name would you give it?

192

If you could put anything you wanted—large or small—in your backyard, what would you put there? (Example: A big merry-go-round.)

193

Who would you say is the most famous person you've ever met?

194

If you could completely eliminate one month from the year, which month would you want to be rid of forever?

195

If you were going to be in a talent show at your school, what would you do on-stage to entertain your friends?

196

If you could get out of school for a week and instead had to spend those five days helping an adult at their job, whose job would you want to help out with during that week?

197

What are some of the many things you enjoy doing for fun that kids who grew up 100 years ago couldn't do? What do you think they did back then for fun?

IMAGINATION IGNITER

198

If you had a gigantic tree in your yard and were asked to design the best treehouse ever, what would the treehouse look like when it was completed?

199

If you could spend one week sleeping on or in anything other than a standard bed, what would you want to try sleeping on? (Example: An inflatable raft in a swimming pool.)

200

Instead of reindeer, what type of animal would you like to see pulling Santa's sleigh?

201

If you could create a new rule that all the kids at your school would be expected to follow, what rule would it be?

202

If you could start your own company today—one that would be run entirely by kids—what would your business make and sell?

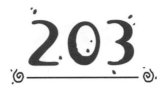

203

If you could become a part of any TV family, which family would you want to join?

204

If you had to spend a week studying something in nature, what in the wild would you want to study?

205

If you could create an all-new Olympic sport or event, what would it be?

206

If you could have any round object in the world, what would you want?

207

If you were a toothbrush designer and had to come up with a brand-new toothbrush that was really unique, what features would it have?

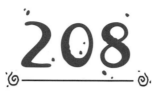

208

If you could get anything back that you either lost or was broken, what would it be?

209

What has been the biggest change in your life during the last year?

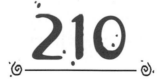

210

If lawns could grow in another color besides green, what color would you want the grass in people's yards to be?

211

What is one really nice thing you could do for a teacher to make her or him happy?

212

If you could build a tunnel from underneath your home to any one destination of your choice, where would your tunnel go?

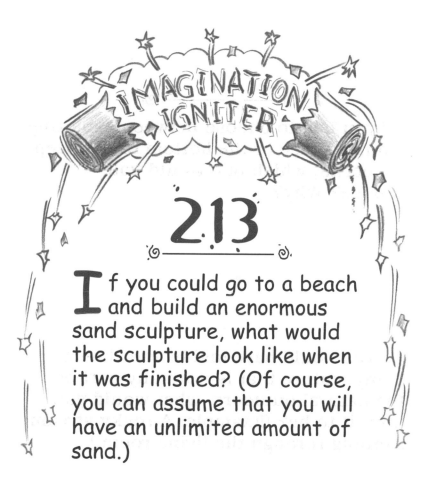

IMAGINATION IGNITER

213

If you could go to a beach and build an enormous sand sculpture, what would the sculpture look like when it was finished? (Of course, you can assume that you will have an unlimited amount of sand.)

214

If you had to choose between exploring outer space or the bottom of the deepest ocean, which one would you choose? Why?

215

If you could have inside your home any feature that is normally part of the natural outdoors, what would you want it to be? (Example: A rocky stream running through the living room.)

216

If you and your friends wanted to have a secret hiding or meeting place somewhere in your neighborhood or town, where would the place be?

217

If you could create your own part for a school play, what type of character would you want to be when you're up on the stage?

218

If you had to fill a large TV-sized box with brand-new toys for a kid whose parents couldn't afford to buy toys for their child, what type of things would you put in the box?

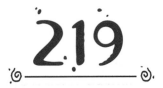

219

If you were in charge of planning a party for your school classmates, what would you choose as the theme for the party, what would you serve to eat, and what type of activities or games would you plan?

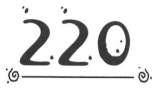

220

If you could bring to life any imaginary creature, or bring back to life any animal that is now extinct, which creature/animal would you choose?

221

If you could personally meet one movie star, whom would you want to meet?

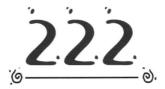

222

If you were keeping a journal of all the fun things you've done so far during your life, what are three things that you would definitely include in the journal?

Got a question of your own that you'd like to send us? How about giving us your answer to one or more of the questions in this book? We'd love to hear from you. Write us a letter, put it in the mail, and we'll be sure to get it...as long as you address it as follows:

Bret and Paul, The Question Guys™
P.O. Box 340
Yankton, South Dakota 57078

Thanks for taking the time to write us, and always keep asking questions!

About the Authors

Bret Nicholaus and Paul Lowrie, The Question Guys™, are the authors of the national bestselling question books *The Conversation Piece* and *The Christmas Conversation Piece*. Altogether, they have written over 3,000 questions that have appeared in ten books. This is their first question book written specifically for kids. Nicholaus and his family live in the Chicago area; Lowrie divides his time between St. Paul, Minnesota and South Dakota.

Matthew 5:16